What People Are Saying About The Great Math Experience By Andrew Field

"-- Most delightful and enjoyable – certainly conducive to 'fun' problem solving. Certainly, an effective teacher will find [the problems] valuable."

Dr. Harry Wong
Author of *The First Days of School*

"Andrew Field has put together a thought provoking collection of problems that are sure to engage your typical middle school classroom. 'The Great Math Experience' draws on Field's experience and provides valuable tips and discussion ideas that will be useful to teachers at all levels."

Dr. Arthur Benjamin
Author of *Mathemagics* and
The Art of Mental Calculation series
Math Department Chair, Harvey Mudd College

"Field uses a comfortable style, mixing personal experience with sound teaching techniques, to engage readers with classic problems in a manner that will help middle-schoolers feel 'at home' with reasoning – a challenge that deserves all the attention we can muster."

Dr. William Speer
UNLV professor and past president of the School Science and Mathematics Association

Here's what others have said about Mr. Field's teaching:

"Wonderful Teaching! You make learning fun and understandable by using real life situations and hands on activities! Great job!"

Lacey Benoit
McNeese State University education student

"I enjoyed the student enthusiasm and interest!"

Pat Gillan
Retired teacher and
Northwestern State University Professor

"You really get the students to think!!!!! I love this class!"

Kalinda Rogers
McNeese State University education student

"I wish I would have had a math teacher like you!"

Susan K. Holmes
McNeese State University education student

"I love how the class is very comfortable asking questions."

Ta'Nisha Clark
McNeese State University education student

"Children are involved!"

Rachel Woodward
McNeese State University education student

The Great Math Experience:

Engaging Problems for Middle School Mathematics

Andrew Field

www.thegreatmathexperience.com

A cataloguing record for this book that includes the U.S. Library of Congress Classification number, the Library of Congress Call number and the Dewey Decimal cataloguing code is available from the National Library of Canada. The complete cataloguing record can be obtained from the National Library's online database at: www.nlc-bnc.ca/amicus/index-e.html
ISBN: 1-4120-1509-x

TRAFFORD

This book was published *on-demand* in cooperation with Trafford Publishing.
On-demand publishing is a unique process and service of making a book available for retail sale to the public taking advantage of on-demand manufacturing and Internet marketing. **On-demand publishing** includes promotions, retail sales, manufacturing, order fulfilment, accounting and collecting royalties on behalf of the author.

Suite 6E, 2333 Government St., Victoria, B.C. V8T 4P4, CANADA
Phone   250-383-6864   Toll-free 1-888-232-4444 (Canada & US)
Fax   250-383-6804   E-mail sales@trafford.com
Web site www.trafford.com   TRAFFORD PUBLISHING IS A DIVISION OF TRAFFORD
HOLDINGS LTD.
Trafford Catalogue #03-1887   www.trafford.com/robots/03-1887.html

10   9   8   7   6   5   4   3

Dedication

To my wonderful wife. How could I have done this without you?

Acknowledgements

Special thanks to:

Lieutenant Anthony Virgadamo for his excellent illustrations of the ball balance problem.

My students at Oak Park, Molo, and Reynaud Middle Schools in Lake Charles, Louisiana and Lakeview Junior High School in Campti, Louisiana for your input on each of these problems.

Dr. William Kritsonis of McNeese State University for encouraging and inspiring me to write the book.

Mike Mire, my assistant principal at Oak Park Middle School, for recognizing and fostering my teaching style.

Dianna Manning for her fantastic cover design.

Contents

Introduction

Like many teachers, I've spent hours on the internet, searching for lesson plans and ideas. It occurred to me after only a few years teaching that I had the lesson plan mastered; what I was searching for was an idea to fill my lesson plan.

Schools and districts vary. Some are rigid in their guidelines for lesson plans, some have no requirement. Some have certain items they require in their lesson plan, others demand only that a teacher has a lesson plan.

I found that no matter what was required of me on paper, the actual lesson was the hard part. Once I had an activity or challenging math problem that met my objective, it was easy to insert that into my lesson plan format.

This book is a compilation of lesson plan ideas. Please don't hope to open it and begin teaching from it. Use these ideas as a base for your own lesson plan.

Each of these problems has been used in my own classroom with great success. Each lists what areas of mathematics you may address by using that problem. Additionally, each problem contains a lot of details about how this problem was received in the classroom. I have tried to make the problems as grade-immaterial as possible; that is, any teacher from about grades 5 to 9 should be able to use most of these problems.

Some problems may be too challenging or too easy for your students. I have included suggestions for simplifying them or for making them more difficult at times.

Generally, I've found that these problems make great lessons when you assign the students some time to work on it, then let them share their ideas either in writing or verbally with the class, allowing them to comment and build upon the ideas of others.

This book is intended to be used as a resource by both beginning and veteran teachers. If you want to photocopy the illustrations for use on your worksheets, please do so.

The problems herein are designed to be used in a non-traditional type lesson. Depending on your students' abilities, the effect of these problems is maximized by group interaction, either via class discussion or cooperative learning. The problems are not designed to replace traditional learning, but to enhance it. All students need "kill and drill" type practice in mathematics. They also need enriching, interesting problems.

I have personally experienced students who transform from math-haters to math lovers, largely due to these types of problems and the discourse they stimulate.

Use this book as a resource. Write all over the margins. Copy pages for your lessons. Modify the numbers for your classes. Do whatever you need to do to make these problems work for you.

I hope that you enjoy them. More importantly, I hope your students do. Maybe for the first time, they'll have a great math experience!

Andrew Field
February 2004

Problem #1
The Ball Balance Problem

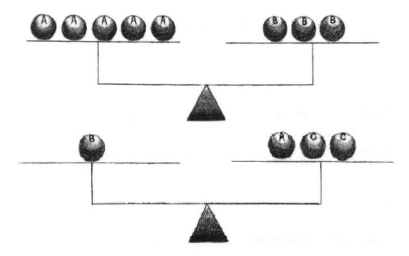

In the illustration, the two scales are balanced. How many "C" balls does it take to balance one "A" ball?

Skills students might use to solve this problem:

Adding/Subtracting fractions, decimals, and/or percents

Substitution property of equality

Distributive property of multiplication

Multiplicative Inverse (reciprocal) property of multiplication

Solving equations

Solving systems of equations

Common multiples

Suggestions.

This is a rich problem that is a wonderful introduction to algebra. I have used it many times with middle schoolers and have been amazed at how they can solve this problem with absolutely no formal training in algebra. Usually, I assign this problem overnight before we get into equations. When the students return, I have them form small groups (no larger than 3 or 4) and discuss their solutions. I then have someone from each group share with the rest of the class. Finally, for the graded assignment, I have each student write a written explanation of their solution. This way, even if the student could not solve the problem initially, he or she should now have a wonderful grasp of it and of several different solutions.

Another possible activity is to have the groups record their solutions on butcher paper and have them present to the class. Sometimes it is fun to hang the solutions up on the wall in various locations and allow the students a few minutes to tour the classroom, then reflect in writing or verbally about each group's work. If your classroom is technological enough, instead of recording the solution on butcher paper, the students can do so in a presentation on a computer. This is often a great way to teach kids how to integrate text and shapes together.

Personal Experience.

I have seen two major solutions to this problem. The first is rarely used by younger students, but is usually the method of choice for high schoolers and above:

If a "B" ball weighs the same as an "A" ball and two "C" balls, then any "B" ball can be replaced with an "A" ball and two "C" balls (an ACC combination) anytime it is convenient. Hence, if you replace all of the "B" balls on the top scale with ACC combinations, you have a scale with five "A" balls on the left side, and three "A" balls and six "C" balls, or ACC ACC ACC, on the right side:

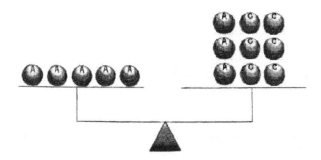

The three "A" balls on the right side weigh the same as three of the "A" balls on the left side, which means that the six "C" balls on the right side must weigh the same as the remaining two "A" balls on the left side.

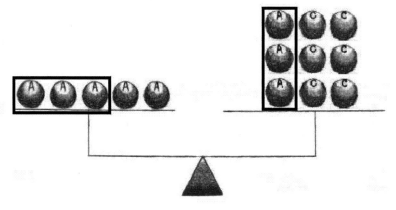

If six "C" balls weigh the same as two "A" balls, then one can see that three "C" balls will balance one "A" ball.

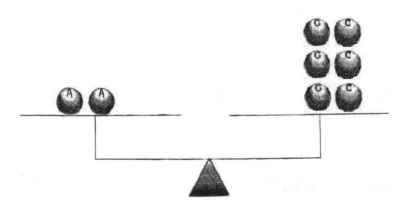

The solution seen more frequently in middle and upper elementary school is that students will substitute a number for the weight of either the "A" or "B" ball and fill in the rest of the weights for the remaining balls. Surprisingly, this will work for any numbers. The rich part of the activity occurs in the discussion. Many students will try several numbers until they find some that will "work". For instance, a student may substitute the value 7 for the A ball:

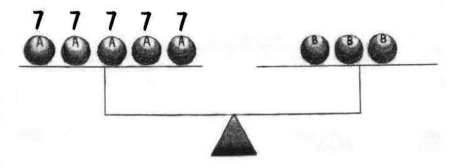

Realizing that each side of the scale must weigh 35 units, the student often will decide that 35/3 either doesn't work or is too cumbersome a calculation to use. This is great because it gives the student a real use for a divisibility rule and it offers the student ownership of the problem: Once the child realizes that the value he or she has chosen is not suitable, he or she chooses to try another solution.

Many students end up with good, easy whole numbers like 3 for the A ball and 5 for the B:

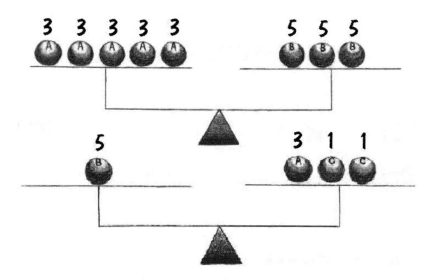

Therefore, each "C" ball weighs one unit and it would take three of them to balance a 3-unit "A" ball.

There are many other easy combinations of numbers, all multiples of the ones shown.

Other students will use this same method but fearlessly tackle the fractions head-on. Some will use decimals or percents. Allowing these methods to surface during a discussion allows those students who are afraid of fractions a chance to realize that they aren't so bad. After all, if their peers could use fractions to solve the problem, it can't be too difficult. Additionally, these students get a chance to refresh their knowledge of fraction operations by watching and listening to someone besides the teacher.

The reason that any number (including fractions) works is easily understood by students who have learned how to solve systems of equations. If 5a=3b and b = a+2c, one can replace b in the first equation with a+2c:

$$5a = 3b$$
$$5a = 3(a+2c)$$

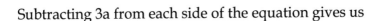

Using the distributive property, we know that

$$5a = 3a + 6c$$

Subtracting 3a from each side of the equation gives us

$$2a = 6c$$

Dividing each side of the equation by two gives us

$$a = 3c$$

So, for any numbers, a will always equal 3c.

If the students are stumped, a good question to lead them is, "Which ball is heaviest? How much heavier is it than the others?" This often leads them to realize that since 3 "B" balls outweigh 5 "A" balls, then the "A" ball is 3/5 of the weight of the "B" ball. Some will realize that the "B" ball is 5/3, or 1 1/3 the weight of the "A" ball, which yields a wonderful insight into reciprocals.

Leading Questions:

> Why did you choose to use that number in the place of the "A" ball?
> How do you know that the "C" ball must weigh 1 pound?
> Does anyone here have a question about the way Susan found the weight of the "B" ball?
> I see some confused looks over in that area. Can you explain it so that this group will understand it?
> Does anyone here think they can rephrase what Jim just said?
> What do you mean, you just replaced BBB with ACC ACC ACC? Can you do that?
> Who agrees with Derek? Who disagrees? Zach, why do you disagree?
> Hang on. Are you saying that 3/5 times 5 is 3? How?

Extension.

Construct a similar problem using a scale that will work with whole numbers. Construct one that won't. Construct one that has balls with unknown weights like this problem, but also include a ball with a known weight.

Problem #2
The Water Hose Problem

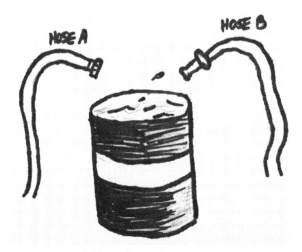

Hose A can fill a bucket in 45 minutes. Hose B can do the same in 30 minutes. How long will it take both hoses together to fill the bucket?

Skills students might use to solve this problem:

Adding fractions with unlike denominators
Adding fractions with like denominators
Reducing fractions
Finding least common multiple

Suggestions.
This problem affords students the opportunity to really understand what fractions mean and get a real

sense of common multiples and how to use them in the context of problem solving.

Contrast the following types of problems that we see so often: What is the LCM of 45 and 30? What is $1/45 + 1/30$?

Personal Experience.

Students' first reaction is almost always to add 45 and 30 to get 75 minutes. Often, they will be satisfied with the answer. It seems to make sense; after all, haven't they been taught that the word "together" is a clue word for addition? The question a teacher can ask to steer students into a more sensible view is, "Which hose can fill the bucket faster?"

Students then will usually disagree. Given a minute or so, they will convince each other that Hose B can fill the bucket faster. Many students have the misconception that more minutes means a faster time. Once they have established that Hose B is faster, students who initially came up with 75 minutes as the answer will want to change it. Some students may even volunteer the idea that the answer has to be less than 30 minutes, if you ask for observations.

The next reaction is to subtract 45 and 30 to get 15 minutes. Now is a good time if you haven't already taught students to do so to have them estimate the answer. Having done this, most students will agree that 15 minutes seems reasonable. Already, without too much deep discussion or mathematical computation, you've established or reinforced quite a few real concepts:

Lower numbers are better when you are talking about time. It always helps to estimate an answer. Your first reaction might not always be correct.

Even though 15 minutes seems reasonable, you should encourage students to check their answer. "Can you always subtract the two hoses' times and get the answer? Can you think of two other hoses with different speeds? Does subtraction work or not?" If you allow every student to create a problem just like this one, but with different times, many will come up with counterexamples to the subtraction method. For example, Hose A can fill the bucket in 1 minute (which is very fast). Hose B can do it in 15 minutes. Is Hose B actually going to slow Hose A down so it takes 14 minutes to fill the bucket?

I usually allow the students to work in groups at this point. They have enough background information to prevent them from making major conceptual errors and their combined brains can usually come up with part of a solution. If not, after a few minutes, I stop the group work and have each group share with the class what they have come up with.

Often, a group can offer part of a solution that will trigger another group or student to build upon it. For example, "We can't find the answer, but we do know that it takes Hose B 15 minutes to fill 1/2 of the bucket." This seems at first to be of little help until another group builds upon it to discover that it takes Hose B 10 minutes to fill 1/3 of the bucket and it takes 5 minutes to fill 1/6 of the bucket and it takes 1 minute to fill 1/30 of the bucket.

Eventually, the groups will realize (either through their own thinking or from teacher-led discussion) that they will have to add 1/45 and 1/30 to find out how much of the bucket will fill in one minute. Of course, the two fractions have to be converted to 2/90 and 3/90 and their sum is 5/90, which is 1/18. If the two hoses can fill 1/18 of the bucket in a minute, in two minutes they can fill 2/18, in three minutes they can fill 3/18, in eighteen minutes they can fill 18/18, or the whole bucket.

Leading Questions:

> Is there a way to draw a model of the problem?
> Can you always subtract the two hoses' times and get the answer?
> Can you think of two other hoses with different speeds? Does subtraction work or not?
> Can you explain that in a different way?
> What makes you think that?

Extension.

Have students model the fractions using graph paper or another manipulative.

Have students write their own hose and bucket problem that will come out with a whole number as its answer.

Have students write a written explanation of the solution to the problem so that a younger child would understand.

14   Andrew Field

Picture by Sarena Senegal, 7th Grade, Oak Park Middle School, Lake Charles, Louisiana 2002

Problem #3
Bunnies and Hutches

There are some bunnies and some hutches. If one bunny is placed in each hutch, then one bunny will be left without a hutch. If two bunnies are placed in each hutch, then one hutch will have only one bunny in it. How many bunnies and hutches are there?

Skills students might use to solve this problem:

Guess and Check
Translating verbal expressions into algebraic expressions
Solving equations and systems of equations
Substitution property of equality
Transitive property of equality

Suggestions.
This problem is easily solved by students in lower elementary grades, but also has deep meaning for students in algebra and pre-algebra.

Most students, if they decide to guess and check, will arrive at the answer quickly because the answer is small. It is important to encourage any level of students to verify their work. It is wonderful to see a child use a model (often a cute picture of bunnies and hutches) and stand up and defend his or her answer.

Personal Experience.

Higher level students can be challenged by writing an algebraic expression for the number of bunnies in relation to the number of hutches. If the class shares, there are often 10 or more attempts at an algebraic expression.

Left in small groups, students can formulate their expressions, test them, argue for or against them, and arrive with some that work.

If one bunny is placed in each hutch, then one bunny will be left without a hutch. This means that the number of bunnies is one greater than the number of hutches, or that the number of hutches is one less than the number of bunnies. This can be written algebraically as $b=h+1$ or $h = b-1$.

If two bunnies are placed in each hutch, then one hutch will have only one bunny in it. This sentence is a little tougher than the first. This means that each hutch except one has two bunnies in it, or that the number of hutches times two (for the two bunnies in each hutch) and minus one (for the one missing bunny in the last hutch) equals the number of bunnies. Algebraically, $b=2h-1$. Or, the number of hutches is half of the number of bunnies plus one. Algebraically, $h = (b+1)/2$.

The transitive property of equality says that if $a=b$ and $b=c$, then $a = c$. The substitution property of equality says that if $a=b$, then a may be substituted for b any time.

If $b=h+1$ and $b = 2h-1$, these properties say that $h+1 = 2h -1$. Solving this equation yields $h=2$. If there are 2 hutches, then students can quickly deduce that there are 3 bunnies.

Extension.

An extension for this problem that allows older students to really explore it in depth is to have them write a new bunny and hutch problem with more bunnies and hutches and have their classmates solve them. For example:

There are some bunnies and some hutches. If you put one bunny in each hutch, there will be three bunnies left without a hutch. If you put three bunnies in each hutch, there will be a hutch with only two bunnies in it.

An older student may still get this problem with guess-and-check methods, but should be encouraged to try to solve it algebraically:

$$b = h + 3$$
$$b = 3h - 1$$

$$h + 3 = 3h - 1$$
$$4 = 2h$$
$$2 = h$$

There are two hutches, so there must be five bunnies.

Problem 4
The Dot Problem

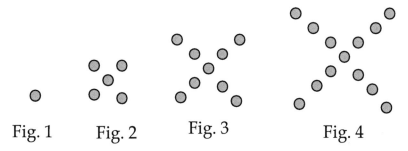

Fig. 1   Fig. 2   Fig. 3   Fig. 4

Draw the 5th figure in this sequence.

How many dots are in the 23rd figure?

How many dots are in the 98th figure?

How many dots are in the nth figure?

Skills students might use to solve this problem:

Finding patterns
Solving equations
Distributive property of multiplication
Simplifying expressions

Personal Experience.

This problem is what algebra is all about! I saw a video of a teacher in Japan teaching this to 6th graders and have used it myself in 7th and 8th grade.

There are two kinds of patterns: recursive and explicit. I actually introduce these two words so the students can speak with a more sophisticated vocabulary.

Both types of patterns are useful, but the explicit pattern is hardest to find.

Most kids will immediately spot the recursive pattern: "It goes up by four every time." Most kids can even point out where the four are: "The four outside dots." "An extra set of four on the legs of the X.."

Our textbooks often encourage students to ignore this recursive pattern and find "the rule" or the explicit pattern, but recursive patterns are very useful, especially in computer programming.

Here's the question that illustrates the need to find an explicit pattern: "What do you need to know in order to find how many dots are in a figure if you are using a recursive formula?" Of course, you need to know how many dots are in the previous figure.

The fun part here is when they have found the explicit pattern.

There are a couple of ways that I have seen students look at the pattern. Using n as the figure number, the number of dots in a figure can be written as:

$$4(n-1) + 1$$

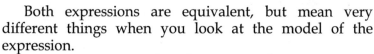

or

$$4n-3$$

Both expressions are equivalent, but mean very different things when you look at the model of the expression.

Here are some samples of written student work:

Kayla:
I can find the number of dots in any figure by first looking at the number. Decrease the figure number by 1, multiply by 4, and add1 to it. I realized that adding 4 would just take all day. I realized that one dot only adds to the outer dots, so the center dot wouldn't be no use yet. After I add all the outer dots the sum is always even. I divided the sum by each row of dots there were, which was 4. I knew that the only way for me to make a situation right is to put back what I took away. So in this case I put back the center dot so that the sequence would be accurate.

Kayla obviously has an idea of what is happening to the outer dots and the constant center dot, but struggles to put it into words. She indicates in her second sentence that she knows the formula. In the mathematics classroom of yesterday, the formula would be enough. What we should be looking for now is the student's grasp of what each piece of the formula means.

Oshe':
You can find the number of dots in any figure by adding the # of dots in the previous figure or figures to the product of however many figures you need to get to that certain figure and four. Example: 5th figure to the 10th figure you have 5 more figures to lead up to the 10th figure, because 5+5=10. So you would count 5 figures more to get to the 10th figure. You would multiply 5x4 because of the figures leading to the 10th figure and the four for the pattern of 4 dots added to each figure. 5x4=20   20+17=37 so there are 37

*dots in figure 10 and I added 17 because
there are 17 dots in figure 5.*

Oshe's explanation led the class to discover the relationship between explicit and recursive patterns. She knows that you must add four each time. As long as you know how many times you need to add four and have a starting place (in her example, she started on figure 5), you can find the number of dots in any figure. A class discussion led another student to use this same technique starting with figure 1. For example, to find the number of dots in figure 10, you will have to add 4 nine times to the amount of dots in figure 1, which is 1. This is the formula $4(n-1) + 1$ that many students come up with. Oshe's example uses the formula $4(n-5)+17$, although she doesn't state this. Notice that both formulas simplify to $4n-3$.

*Jade: You multiply 4 times whatever figure
number you are working on. For example, if
you are working on the 21st problem you
multiply 21x4. Then you subtract three
because you used the center dot too many
times.*

Jade looks at the problem from a different standpoint. She counts the center dot in each leg of the "x" shape, so she can multiply the figure number by 4. Then she subtracts three for the three extra times she counted the center dot. A teacher question like "What is the algebraic formula that represents Jade's method?" will get the result $4n-3$. The great things to point out here: 1) There are many ways to solve a problem, and 2) The simplest form of the expression may not be the best way to describe how you got the answer. In Jade's case, it was. In Kayla's, it wasn't.

> *Joseph: You can find the number of dots in any*
> *figure by multiply the figure number times*
> *four and then subtract three, If you don't*
> *believe me, try it.*
> *If you end up with an even number, it is wrong.*

Joseph, while confident, fails to communicate his thinking beyond the formula. However, he makes an interesting observation in his postscript. Things like this shouldn't be ignored. Bring them out so the whole class can learn. A younger class could benefit just from the discussion that would arise from the results of adding even and odd numbers. A more advanced class almost always has a student or two who can benefit from a 2-minute digression as another student quickly explains his thinking:

> *Teacher: Joseph, why do you say that if you end*
> *up with an even number, it's wrong?*
> *Joseph: Well, all of the answers are odd, so I*
> *figured none of them could be even. Also, you*
> *start with one and you add four every time.*
> *An odd plus an even is always odd.*
> *Teacher: Always? Does anyone disagree? Can*
> *anyone find a counterexample? Take a*
> *minute or two and see.*

After about sixty seconds, the class is murmuring in agreement that an odd plus an even is always odd. Some have even tried it with negative numbers.

Problem 5
The Wire-Cutting Problem

A wire factory makes wires that are bent six times like the one shown above. If the wire is cut like this:

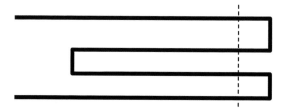

How many pieces will there be? How many pieces will there be on the second cut?

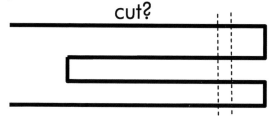

The third? The 10th? 100th? The nth? Assume that all cuts remain to the right of the 3rd bend.

Skills students might use to solve this problem:

Finding patterns
Solving equations
Distributive property of multiplication
Simplifying expressions

Suggestions.
This problem is extremely similar to the Dot Problem. It illustrates the different ways of looking at similar patterns, and I almost always use it immediately after the Dot problem. You might want to use both problems, or only one of them.
Personal Experience.
A common misconception here is that there are only three pieces on the first cut. I thought this the first time I saw the problem, too, because I was looking at the wire not as a long, skinny, bent piece of wire, but as a thick, U-shaped piece of metal somewhat akin to a tuning fork:

Actually, there are five pieces on the first cut. Each cut adds four more pieces to the total, which makes it very similar to the Dot Problem. However, in the Dot Problem, figure 1 had only one dot, and in the Wire Cutting Problem, figure 1 has 5 pieces.
Algebraically, the two problems are similar in that they have the same rate of change, which is the slope of the equation. They are different because they have a

different starting point, which is the y-intercept of the equation.

Students who have progressed beyond concrete models to abstract formulas can often find that there are 5 pieces in the first figure, 9 pieces in the next, 13 in the next, and so on, so they quickly find that if you multiply the cut number by 4 and add 1, you know the number of pieces. The formula for the number of pieces on any given cut can be written as 4c +1, where c is the number of cuts.

However, when pressed to show in a picture where the 4 and the 1 are, students often come across some difficulty. They know that the 4 has to do with the groups of 4 that get added on each cut, but don't understand how the 1 fits into the picture.

This is a wonderful time to introduce the words variable and constant if you haven't already. There are obviously some pieces of the wire that are there every time. Those pieces are represented in the formula by a numeral, or constant. There are some pieces that might be there or might not, depending on the cut. These pieces come in groups of four and the number of groups varies, hence the term variable.

In actuality, 5 is a constant in this problem, even though the formula simplifies to 4c+1.

A more accurate formula is 4(c-1) +5. It is worthwhile to let students discuss how these two formulas are alike and how they are different. Obviously, they're alike because they yield the same number; in fact, one simplifies into the other. They are different because they represent two different ways of looking at the problem. Watching kids struggle to find where the extra group of four comes from is rewarding.

This problem ties in well with graphing and with the concepts of slope and y-intercept as well. Even if you do this problem before you teach graphing, you can reintroduce it at the beginning of the graphing unit.

Picture by Nahari Levine, 8th Grade, Molo Middle School, Lake Charles, Louisiana

Problem #6
The Locker Problem

A middle school has an enrollment of 1000 students. The school has 1000 lockers, numbered 1 to 1000, one for each student. On Monday morning, all 1000 lockers are closed and all 1000 students are outside. The first student enters and opens all of the lockers. The second student follows and closes every second locker, beginning with the second locker. The third student enters the school and reverses every third locker beginning with locker number 3 (that is, if a locker is open, she closes it and if it is closed, she opens it). This procedure continues until all 1000 students have entered the building and passed by all the lockers. When they are done, which lockers will be open? Which lockers will have been opened and shut only once?

Skills and concepts students might use to solve this problem:

Squares
Primes
Factors, multiples
Multiplying and dividing
Divisibility rules

Suggestions.
This is a problem that shows up everywhere. For younger students, you may want to say that the school has only 100 lockers. Older students should realize after some thinking that they could simplify this problem themselves. Working a simpler problem is one of the most useful problem-solving techniques.

Older students may work well alone on this problem, while younger ones may need to work in groups.

Personal Experience.
A technique that I found to be effective is to allow the students five minutes at first in dead silence to work on this problem alone. They need this time so they can begin to construct a model of the problem if they need it. Also, sometimes kids just need a few minutes to warm their brains up.

After the five minutes, I ask if anyone has any observations they want to share. There is almost always something someone has figured out. A student may have noticed that the first locker will definitely be open. Another may have noticed that the prime numbers will open and shut only once. If your students are comfortable with the definition of prime numbers, then they may spot this quickly.

The answer is that the lockers with square numbers will be open because only square numbers have an odd number of factors. For example, locker number 1 will obviously still be open. The number 1, which is a square number, has an odd number of factors. Conversely, the number 2, which is not a square number, has two factors, 1 and 2. The number 4, which is a square number, has 3 factors, 1, 2, and 4. The number 100, which is a square number, has an odd number of factors. It has nine factors: 1, 2, 4, 5, 10, 20, 25, 50, and 100.

Some of the lockers in the problem will be opened many times. For example, by the time the 25th student has entered school, locker number 72 has been opened and closed 8 times already.

The power of this problem lies in its contributions to number sense. Although the ability to quickly realize that square numbers have odd numbers of factors and that prime numbers have only two factors is useful in math competitions, most of our students are not math competitors. The benefit they receive from this problem is a chance to look hard at many different facets of mathematics: factors, common factors, multiples, common multiples, multiplication, division, primes, squares, etc. And they get to look at it in a way that keeps you, the teacher, from standing on the stage and spouting it out, which keeps both you and the students from doing any real thinking.

If you must lecture, do it in spurts during this problem and the discussion that it spurs, but ask yourself: Do I need to stand up and say this? Or can I ask a couple of questions and get a student to say it?

> *Teacher: Has anyone made any interesting observations?*
> *Derrick: The doors that open and shut only once can only be divided by one and the same number.*
> *Teacher: The same number as what?*
> *Derrick: The same number as the locker.*

Teacher: I think I know what you're talking about, but I'm getting confused looks from the table next to you. Can you say that in a way that will help Justin understand?

Derrick: Uhh, like seven can only be divided by one and by seven, so that locker will only open and shut once.

Teacher: Does anyone remember what this kind of number is called? Jaime?

Jaime: Odd numbers.

Teacher: Michael?

Michael: It can't be odd numbers because 2 only can be divided by 1 and 2. And 2 is even.

Teacher: Who agrees with Michael? Who agrees with Jaime? Who's still not sure? That's OK.

Jaime: Oh yeah, and it can't be odd numbers because 9 is an odd number and it can be divided by 3.

Teacher: That's a good counterexample. Can anyone give another?

Harmony: 15.

Teacher: Is 15 a counterexample to Jaime's statement that not all odd numbers are divisible by only 1 and themselves? Who thinks so? Who thinks not? Who still isn't too sure? That's OK. So a number that is divisible by only 1 and itself isn't called an odd number. Who remembers what it's called?

Tiffany: Com...com...

Justin: Compound numbers!

Tawana: Composite numbers! (lots of shouts of agreement)

Charmayne: No, no, it's prime numbers.

Teacher: Where did you get prime from com-com-compound-composite?

> *Charmayne: Prime is the opposite of composite.*
> *Nikia: Yeah, it's prime.*
> *Teacher: Is it?*
> *Justin (looking up from glossary in textbook):*
>   *Yeah, it is.*

If no one can remember (or no one has ever learned) the definition of prime numbers, then you ought to tell them now. Make them write it down. Make them write it in their own words. Make them describe it in their journals, or whatever you want, but don't just tell them once and let it go. The activity up until this point has been interesting and the students have discovered prime numbers. Give them ownership of the definition and they'll never forget it, even 10 years after college.

Some students have trouble finding all of the factors of a number because they do not go about the task systematically. For example, to find all of the factors of 100, which is a fairly familiar number, many students will begin to list: 50 and 2, 25 and 4, 10 and 10. Inevitably, someone leaves some factors out.

If they don't already use this technique, I like to share my own personal technique of factoring numbers with my students somewhere during this lesson. I call it factoring from the outside in. I make students write this down in their notebook or math toolkit. Mathematics is not a spectator sport; students won't learn just by watching their teacher write.

For example, to factor the number 72, I start with 72 and its two most obvious factors, written with quite a bit of space between them:

Factors of 72:
1,   72

Then I proceed to the next factor of 72, which is 2. If the students don't get why we choose two next, it may be time to learn divisibility rules. The divisibility rules, which are printed at the end of this section in a table, ought to go in students' notebooks as well.

Factors of 72:
1, 2,   36, 72

Next comes 3, since 72 is divisible by three. If students don't know what 72 divided by 3 is, that's OK. Encourage them to scribble it out quickly in the margin or on some scratch paper.

Factors of 72:
1, 2, 3,   24, 36, 72

Next we try 4. Is 72 divisible by 4? The divisibility rule isn't much help if you're a middle schooler who doesn't know the multiplication facts past 12x4=48. Some students may realize that if you count by fours you will get to 72 because it is 8 less than 80, which is definitely divisible by 4. Again, if students don't know what 72 divided by 4 is, then have them work it out. It's OK not to know the answer; but it's not OK to just leave the problem unsolved.

Factors of 72:
1, 2, 3, 4, 18, 24, 36, 72

Next comes 5, which obviously doesn't go into 72. Students who know their multiplication facts past 10 should see that 6 will go into 72 twelve times.

Factors of 72:
1, 2, 3, 4, 6,   12, 18, 24, 36, 72

7 doesn't work, but 8 does:

Factors of 72:
1, 2, 3, 4, 6, 8, 9, 12, 18, 24, 36, 72

The next number is 9, which we've already used, so our list is complete:

When you factor a square number, there won't be two numbers meeting in the middle, but one, which makes the total number of factors come out to be odd. This is why the lockers with square numbers are the only lockers left open.

Locker 100:
1, 2, 4, 5, 10, 20, 25, 50, 100
o c o c   o   c   o   c   o

Extension.
Who is the last student to touch exactly two lockers? Three? Four?
Who is the first student to touch exactly four lockers?
How many lockers are left open?
If the school did this next year on the first day of school, how many more students and lockers will they

need to have one more locker open at the end of the problem?

Divisibility Rules

2: If a number is divisible by two, it is even. Its last digit must be an even number.

3: If a number is divisible by three, the sum of its digits must be divisible by three.

4: If a number is divisible by 4, the number formed by its last two digits must be divisible by 4.

5: If a number is divisible by 5, its last digit must be 5 or 0.

6: If a number is divisible by 6, it is divisible by both 2 and 3.

7: There are some rules for 7, but none easy enough to memorize. You'll just have to try it.

8: If a number is divisible by 8, the number formed by its last three digits must be divisible by 8.

9: If a number is divisible by 9, the sum of its digits must be divisible by 9.

Picture by Sarena Senegal, 7th Grade, Oak Park
Middle School, Lake Charles, Louisiana

Problem #7
The Tire Rotation Problem

A car is driven 40,000 miles using four tires and a spare tire. The tires are rotated so that each tire travels the same number of miles. What is the number of miles traveled by each tire?

Skills students might use to solve this problem:

Unit rates
Multiplying / dividing

Suggestions.
This is a great problem that older students can solve in less than half an hour. Younger students may need a day or two to solve it. If you assign this problem for homework, you may want to preface the assignment with two things: 1) This is not a trick question, and 2) The answer is not 10,000. This will keep your students from thinking they have solved the problem in 2 seconds.

Personal Experience.
The simple answer is that if the car drove 40,000 miles and it drove the entire distance on 4 tires, then it drove a total "tire-distance" of 160,000 miles. Since all five tires received equal wear, 160,000 divided by five is 32,000 miles traveled by each tire.

My students, who get lots of brainteasers from other teachers, really thought this was a trick question and had lots of suspicious questions. Once they realized that it was straightforward problem, they settled down with trying to do the math.

Kids really struggle with the idea of "tire-distance," which is really a unit rate. It may be useful to point out that if you drive one mile, each tire on the car has driven one mile as well. The front right tire went one mile, the front left tire went one mile, etc. If you add all of the tires together, you have a total of four "tire-miles." I think, however, that it's best to allow the students to work together and lead them into this thinking on their own. Simply inserting a question like, "How many miles did each tire travel?" can lead a student into the solution.

The quick answer many will offer is 10,000 miles. If allowed to present their answer and reasoning without fear of criticism, another student may respectfully disagree by pointing out that if the car went 40,000 miles, then each tire also went 40,000 miles, or, in this case, each tire went a little less than that, since a spare shared the road time with the four tires. The key is providing students with an atmosphere that allows them to speak up without fear.

Another great point to bring up here is that if you have an idea of what the answer will be before you begin any real work on the problem, you'll know if your calculations are wrong. We tell kids over and over and we give them little sheets with the steps of problem solving and we hang the steps of problem solving on the wall and kids almost never remember to estimate the answer before anything else. It's big problems like these that afford teachers an opportunity to point out in context why you should estimate an answer beforehand.

One seventh grader offered this solution:

> I knew there were five tires and that they would get equal wear, so if you stop five times to rotate tires, you'll stop every 8,000 miles. Every tire gets a chance to ride in each position (front left, front right, back left, back

right, and the spare). So that means that every tire gets to go 8,000 miles in each position except the spare, so 8,000 times 4 is 32,000. Each tire travels 32,000 miles.

Anytime a student gets the answer right, it's a chance for other students to analyze it. Don't just say, "That's right! Good job!" Instead, ask, "Who agrees? Why? Who disagrees? Why?" Those two questions will allow other students to share ownership of a solution and to correct inaccuracies in their own solutions, when this would never occur without a chance to voice disagreement.

Students should feel like it's OK to disagree with the correct answer when you're learning. It's not OK to disagree with the correct answer when the lesson is over. It's up to you, the teacher, to foster this kind of environment.

Leading Questions.

How do you know how many miles each tire has traveled?
Can you explain how you arrived at that number?
Why did you choose to divide there?

Extension.
Write a similar problem that will have an answer that doesn't end with a zero. Share it with your classmates.

This problem was in the Countdown Round for the 2000 Chapter Competition of MathCounts.

Problem # 8
Busy Work for Gauss

What is the sum of all the counting numbers from 1 to 100, inclusive?

Skills students might use to solve this problem:

Addition
Compatible numbers
Adding arithmetic sequences

This is a famous math problem that Carl Freidrich Gauss' teacher posed to the class, possibly hoping to keep them busy. Not only did ten-year old Gauss solve this problem quickly, but he did it mentally, writing the answer on his slate and flinging it onto the teacher's desk. The teacher was so impressed that he spent his own money to buy young Carl the best arithmetic textbook he could find, stating that he had nothing left to teach the boy.

Suggestions.

There are many ways to pose this problem to your class.

For older students, tell them Gauss' story and have them try to come up with a technique to answer it mentally as well.

For younger students, it may be useful to allow then to perform at least some, if not all, of the tedious calculations that they believe necessary to solve the problem. There really is no better illustration of the need for compatible numbers than the need to alleviate tiresome, even painful computation.

You may want to write the problem on the board as it is and hope a young Gauss will step up within seconds.

You may want to start with the numbers from 1 to 1000, hoping that students will see that there must be a shortcut – what kind of sadistic teacher would assign this sort of problem if there wasn't a shortcut?

Personal Experience.

Students obviously will moan and groan, asking why in the world they should have to do this. I avoid this by posing the problem within the first two days of school, before the students are comfortable enough with me to complain. It also gives them insight into a famous mathematician and lets them see that math can be interesting.

Students will make countless errors, as will anyone who is adding 100 numbers. This is fine. They are supposed to make errors. Many kids will actually get the answer right, after fifteen minutes of adding. Let them take the time to do it. Fifteen minutes is a relatively small portion of a student's life compared to the combined total they will save once they realize the use of compatible numbers.

One way to solve the problem is to visualize the first 50 numbers lined up from left to right, and the next 50 numbers lined up immediately underneath the first 50 from right to left and offset to the left one space, so that the number 51 is directly beneath the 49, the number 52 is directly beneath the 48, the number 53 is directly beneath the 47, and so on until the number 99 is directly beneath the 1. The number 50 is left without a partner, and so is 100. Each pair of numbers adds to 100 and there are 49 pairs, so those add to 4900. Add the 100 and 50 and you get 5050.

Another way is to line the numbers up similarly, without the offset. Now there are 50 pairs of numbers, each adding to 101:

$$50 \times 101 = 5050$$

You may want to share with a more advanced class how to find the sum of any arithmetic sequence. You use the formula $n(a+z)/2$, where n is the number of terms in the sequence, a is the first term, and z is the last term.
For example, find the sum of $3+6+9+\ldots+27+30$.
There are 10 terms. The first term is 3, the last is 30.
$10(3+30)/2 = 165$.
In our problem, there are 100 terms, the first being 1 and the last being 100.
$100(1+100)/2=5050$.
Leading Questions:

Is there an easier way to do this?
Are there any steps that you can do mentally?

Extension.
Have students find the sum of a different arithmetic sequence. Have advanced students research how to find the sum of any arithmetic sequence and how to use a formula to do so and share it with the class.

$1+2+3+4+5+6+7+8+9+10+11+12+13+14+15+16+17+18$
$+19+20+21+22+23+24+25+26+27+28+29+30+31+32+33+3$
$4+35+36+37+38+39+40+41+42+43+44+45+46+47+48+49+$
$50+51+52+53+54+55+56+57+58+59+60+61+62+63+64+65$
$+66+67+68+69+70+71+72+73+74+75+76+77+78+79+80+8$
$1+82+83+84+85+86+87+88+89+90+91+92+93+94+95+96+$
$97+98+99+100$

Problem # 9
Bippities, Bops, and Boos

Six bippities equal three bops, and six bops equal two boos. How many boos are there in one bippity, one bop and one boo?

Skills students might use to solve this problem:

Adding fractions
Converting fractions
Equivalent fractions

Suggestions.

If there's one thing math students in middle school hate almost universally, it's fractions. In fact, most adults hate them, too. You're going to have to teach them, even if you don't like them. You may as well make them fun, and the discussions that arise from this problem elicit plenty of giggles.

If you are trying to teach problem solving, you may want to let the students begin this problem haphazardly, without defining the real problem. They'll think they've wasted their efforts and it will be up to you to help them realize that their efforts have helped them learn to find their purpose before they begin solving a problem.

On the other hand, you may want to begin with the question, "What is this problem asking you?" This will allow all students to begin with the idea that they must solve everything in terms of boos.

Personal Experience.
As in all word problems, the first thing a student needs to do is figure out exactly what the problem is asking for. Many students, allowed to mentally roam on this one, will figure out all kinds of things that don't help find the answer.
So here's the math of it:

> *One bippity = ½ bop = 1/6 boo*
> *One bop = 2 bippities = 1/3 boo*
> *One boo = 3 bops = 6 bippities*
> *One bippity, one bop, and one boo = 1/6 boo, 1/3 boo, and 1 boo.*
> *1/6 + 1/3 + 1 = 1½*
> *There are 1½ boos in one bippity, one bop, and one boo.*

What will the kids do to solve this one? Kids who are strong in fractional operations (yes, they exist!) will try to solve it in the simplest way possible, which is using the abstract calculations above.
Kids who aren't so comfortable with fractions may want to solve the problem by drawing a model.
Whatever the technique, this problem leaves lots of room for error because of the confusing names of the three units. Having students work in groups to verify their solutions will eliminate most of the unnecessary errors.
Leading Questions.

> What is the relationship between bippities and bops?
> How can this be represented in a picture?
> What if six bops equaled three boos?

Extension.

Have students add a fourth unit of measure to the problem and rewrite the question to include it.

For example:

Six bippities equal three bops, and six bops equal two boos. Four boos equal one bada-bing. How many bippities are in a bop, two boos, and three bada-bings?

THE CRAZY EMPEROR

Picture by Eric Chatman, 8th Grade, Oak Park Middle
School, Lake Charles, Louisiana

Problem #10
The Crazy Emperor

You have been invited to the emperor's banquet. The emperor is a rather strange host. Instead of sitting with his guests at his round dining table, he walks around the table, pouring oats on the head of every other person. If you get oats on your head, you have to leave. He continues this process, pouring oats on the head of every other person who has not had oats until there is only one person left. Where should you sit if you do not want oats on your head?

I usually lead this question off by arranging the students' desk in a big circle. I walk around the room, simulating pouring oats on heads. One way to do this is have students raise their hands when they get oats on their heads, but inevitably some hands go down or don't go high enough and you end up making a mistake. I used colored index cards and laid them on student desks as I passed around the circle. The cards were easy to spot when I made the circuit each successive time.

One thing the students will always ask is, "How many guests are there?" The answer is that it is different every night. You have to come up with a plan so that no matter how many guests arrive, you will be the one without oats on your head.

It is a good idea to demonstrate the emperor's behavior on several different sized groups.

With a group of three guests, the emperor pours oats on Guest 1, skips Guest 2, and pours oats on Guest 3, leaving Guest 2 as the last person. So with three guests, you should sit in seat 2.

With a group of 4 guests, Guests 1 and 3 get it first. The emperor skips Guest 4, then pours oats on Guest 2, leaving Guest 4 as the last person.

With 10 guests, the emperor pours oats on Guests 1,3,5,7, and 9, then skips 10, pours oats on 2, skips 4, pours oats on 6, skips 8, pours oats on 10, skips 4 again, and pours oats on 8, leaving Guest 4 as the last oat-free guest.

It is helpful to allow the students about 10 minutes after the demonstration to work on this problem alone. When I did this, every single student was working. Some were silently counting off something on their fingers, some were drawing models, some had broken the work-by-yourself rule and started arguing quietly with a neighbor. Normally, this would cause me a little consternation, but when I listened, they were arguing about which seat was best!

Some students begin a table, and a couple of others begin a line graph. If you have the means to incorporate computer use into your class, you can create (or, even better, have students create) a list and graph using Microsoft Excel or another similar software.

Number of Guests	Best seat
1	1
2	2
3	2
4	4
5	2
6	4
7	6
8	8
9	2
10	4
11	6
12	8
13	10
14	12
15	14
16	16
17	2
18	4
19	6
20	8
21	10
22	12
23	14
24	16
25	18
26	20
27	22
28	24
29	26
30	28
31	30
32	32

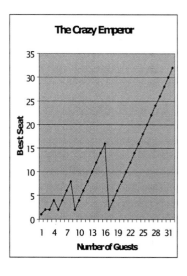

After the students have had time to begin their solutions, a class discussion will usually bring out the observation that the solution has something to do with powers of 2. Someone may point out that the pattern counts by twos but starts over at 2 every now and then.

You may want to give the students overnight to think it over and analyze the pattern further.

The pattern is that the best seat counts by twos until it reaches a power of two, then starts over at 2.

The students may arrive at several solutions:

One is that you find the largest power of 2 that is smaller than the number of guests. Then you subtract that power of 2 from the number of guests and multiply that answer by two to get the number of the best seat.

Another solution is to find the smallest power of 2 that is larger than the number of guests. Then you subtract the number of guests from that power of 2, double that number and subtract that result from the power of 2.

My students had a lot of fun trying to figure out how to write a program for the graphing calculator that would determine the best seat if you input the number of guests. I found that with calculator and computer programs, my visual learners really appreciated seeing a flowchart that illustrated the program.

Another exciting revelation for middle schoolers is that an exponent can be a variable.

Here is the program for the TI-83 graphing calculator:

```
PROGRAM:EMPEROR
:Disp "HOW MANY GUESTS?"
:Input G
:Disp "YOU SHOULD"
:Disp "SIT IN"
:Disp "SEAT NUMBER"
:0→A
```

:Lbl 1
:If 2^A>G
:Goto 2
:If 2^A=G
:Goto 3
:A+1→A
:Goto 1
:Lbl 2
:A-1→A
:Disp (G-2^A)*2
:Goto 4
:Lbl 3
:Disp G
:Lbl 4

```
HOW MANY GUESTS?
?25
YOU SHOULD
SIT IN
SEAT NUMBER
                18
             Done
```

Problem #11
The Platonic Solids

How many polyhedra can you make using only congruent regular polygons as faces?

Skills students might explore:

Measuring linear distance
Measuring angles
Sum of angles in a polygon
Geometry vocabulary

This is more of an exploration than a problem. You can easily spend a whole week on the various facets of this question, to include angle measurements of various polygons, all of the geometric vocabulary, and the platonic solids. I have italicized some vocabulary words that can arise during this activity. There are many more.

With more advanced students, you may want to add the caveat that the same number of faces must meet at each *vertex* and that the shape must be *convex*.

I had great success with this by using foam board, exacto knives, a hole punch, protractors, and twist ties. I spent about $20 on the foam board and got the twist ties from the produce section of a grocery store. I borrowed the knives from the art teacher.

Have the students construct *two-dimensional regular polygons* with side lengths of your choice. I used 6 inches for every polygon, just to show that *triangles* and *hexagons* with 6 inch sides are extremely different in size. Also, many protractors have a 6-inch ruler, so you don't have to use a ruler as a straight edge, which eliminates having to get rulers out and distribute them to students. Before you waste valuable foam board, you may want students to draw these polygons on paper. Begin with a triangle with 6-inch sides. If your students are like mine, they have trouble measuring both inches and *degrees*. Many students want to line up the number 1 on the ruler with the edge of the object they're measuring. After all, you start counting with 1, so shouldn't you start measuring with 1? Unfortunately, this makes the measurement come out as 1 inch shorter than it ought to be.

I usually provide a counterexample to my students by standing at the door and saying,

"I'm going to see how many steps it takes to cross the room." Before I start walking, however, I say, very firmly, "One!" Then, with an exaggerated stepping-off, I begin to step and count, "Two, three, four..." The students usually shout and stop me, so I start over exactly the same way about three times, acting confused that they keep stopping me. Finally, I let a student tell me that I can't count 1 before I even take one step.

I'll ask, "So are you saying that when we count, we really start with zero?"

Although often this isn't enough to make students line up the zero on the ruler on their own, it at least illustrates the need to.

I don't even tell the students that an *equilateral* triangle has 60 degree angles. I don't even tell them that this triangle is equilateral. Invariably, they will draw two 6-inch sides, connected at a vertex, and wonder why they can't fit another 6-inch side between the remaining two *vertices*. Often, they try to sneak it past me, hoping I won't notice in passing that their supposedly equilateral triangle is hopelessly lopsided.

After some frustration, I usually drop the hint, "I gave you a protractor for a reason…" Then, often there is someone in the group who can refresh everyone's memory on how to use a protractor. Have them come to your overhead projector (if you have one) and show everyone. Most protractors are clear so they work great on the overhead.

A classroom discussion at this point could bring up some valuable refreshers:

> *Teacher: So what kind of triangle are we trying to make? Serena?*
>
> *Serena: Equilateral.*
>
> *Teacher: How do we know it's equilateral?*
>
> *Serena: It has three equal sides.*
>
> *Jordan: And three equal angles.*
>
> *Teacher: Three equal angles? Is that true? Does anyone agree with Jordan's statement that an equilateral triangle has three equal angles? (a dozen hands go up) OK, I'll buy that. So if the angles are equal, what are they?*
>
> *PJ: Acute.*
>
> *Teacher: PJ says they're acute. Who agrees? (some hands) Who disagrees? (some hands) Who's not sure? (more hands) Why do you say that, PJ?*
>
> *PJ: Well, you can look at them and tell they're acute. (several students nod in agreement)*
>
> *Teacher: What does acute mean?*
>
> *PJ: Smaller than a right angle, less than 90.*
>
> *Teacher: OK, how acute are they?*
>
> *Ashly: 60 degrees!*
>
> *Teacher: What makes you so sure, Ashly?*
>
> *Joseph: Yeah, what makes you so sure?*

Ashly: Because the angles in a triangle add up to 180 and if all three angles are the same, then 60+60+60 is 180.

Once the 60-degree idea is introduced, all students need to do is figure out how to draw a 60-degree angle. All too often, I find that students have no concept of angle measurement because it is hard to teach! Most textbooks don't have many problems requiring students to draw angles because drawings are hard to grade.

You may have to get down to the basics and teach how to use a protractor (here's where the overhead projector is useful). You may teach a grade where you are supposed to teach protractor use. You may teach a grade where the students should already know how. Regardless of grade level, if they can't use a protractor, you have to teach them.

Students are often interested to find that degrees are degrees, no matter how long the *rays* of an angle are and no matter what "starting point" you use on a protractor. You can draw a 60-degree angle using the zero and 60 mark on the protractor, or the 10 and 70, or the 20 and 80, or so on. As long as the start and end points are 60 degrees apart, you've got a 60 degree angle. You can even start on 180 and end on 120.

Another huge side discussion can arise from having to determine which ring of numbers to use (if you have protractors with two rings of numbers). This invariably leads to a definition of *supplementary angles*.

Now, students can draw a 60-degree angle with 6-inch legs and connect the endpoints for the third side and *voila!* they have an equilateral triangle, which is a regular polygon, *congruent* with all of the other equilateral triangles in the room and *similar* to all of the other equilateral triangles in the world.

Ask students: "Can you make a *polyhedron* using only two of these triangles?" It takes no time to realize that you can't, because for the *space figure* to be closed, the two triangles have to lay flat against each other, which makes them become one triangle. "How about with three?" A little longer time to investigate, and students realize that the answer is no, and they have wonderful reasons for it. If they have made equilateral triangles out of construction paper of any other lightweight paper, they can connect three of them, but only by bending the sides, which makes the shapes become something other than polygons.

Usually, they will realize that three equilateral triangles joined at one vertex and arranged so that their sides touch form an empty *base* that is also an equilateral triangle.

Have them punch holes near the vertices and join four equilateral triangles together with twist ties to form the smallest of the possible solutions, the *tetrahedron*. Four congruent regular triangles can be joined to make this interesting polyhedron, which is also an equilateral *triangular pyramid*.

So everyone (or every group) has a tetrahedron of their own. Hang them from the ceilings and in the hall. People love to see that stuff. Other students will ask their teacher why they don't get to make that stuff.

The next question is, "Can we make any other *polyhedra* using equilateral triangles?"

Someone should have discovered by now that you can lay six triangles joined at one vertex out flat and it makes a big *hexagon*. 6 triangles, 60 degrees each. 6 x 60 = 360. Isn't that cool? If you take one triangle out of the hexagon and join the sides of the remaining 5 triangles, the center vertex raises a little, like a tent. Remove another triangle and join the remaining 4 triangles' sides and the center raises some more. Remove another triangle and you have only 3 triangles joined at a vertex, which is a tetrahedron. Notice that there are 3 equilateral triangles meeting at every vertex of a tetrahedron.

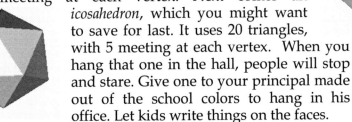

So the next easiest shape to make is an *octahedron*, which uses 8 equilateral triangles with 4 meeting at each vertex. Next comes an *icosahedron*, which you might want to save for last. It uses 20 triangles, with 5 meeting at each vertex. When you hang that one in the hall, people will stop and stare. Give one to your principal made out of the school colors to hang in his office. Let kids write things on the faces.

Let the kids come to the conclusion that there are no more polyhedra that you can make using congruent equilateral triangles.

If they don't come up with the idea on their own, ask, "Is a triangle the only kind of regular polygon?"

Although they will come up with many answers, the next logical polygon is the *square*, which is the only regular *quadrilateral*. If you lay four squares flat, joined at one vertex, they make a bigger square. 4 squares, 90 degrees each. 4 x 90 = 360. Isn't that cool? Remove a square and join the sides of the remaining three squares and the center rises, like a tent. Punch holes and make a polyhedron with three squares meeting at each vertex. This is called a *hexahedron*, or more commonly, a *cube*.

What's next? *Pentagons*, of course. There are several ways to find out the angle measure of a regular pentagon. You can draw lots of *irregular* pentagons and find the sum of their angles and divide by 5. You can make a chart that shows that if you subtract two from the number of sides of a polygon and multiply by 180, you get the angle sum. This is a useful formula, but it may not be where you're going with the lesson.

It's interesting to think about 6 equilateral triangles laying flat to form 360 degrees and about 4 squares laying flat to form 360 degrees and imagine that it will take less than 4 pentagons to do the same. It can't take two pentagons, because that would mean that each angle would be 180 degrees, which is *straight*. It must take three pentagons to form 360 degrees at a shared vertex, which means that 360/3 = 120. However, if you draw 120 degree angles, you get a regular hexagon. If you lay three hexagons out, you get 360 degrees. Remove a hexagon and join the sides of the remaining two hexagons and you get a two-dimensional shape, so we've discovered that congruent regular hexagons can't form a polyhedron.

Pentagons must have an angle measurement between 90 and 120 degrees. Halfway between these two is 105 degrees, but this isn't quite right if you draw it (a valuable observation for kids to make). 108 is the actual measurement, and how long you spend on letting kids discover this and when and if you decide to just tell them is up to you.

Three regular pentagons joined at a vertex can join up with 9 other pentagons to form a *dodecahedron*, which is just as cool-looking as an icosahedron.

That's it! The tetrahedron, hexahedron, octahedron, dodecahedron, and icosahedron are the only 5 polyhedra you can make with congruent regular polygons. They're called *the Platonic Solids* and can be the springboard to many rich investigations and discussions.

On an interesting note, a soccer ball is not a platonic solid because it is made of hexagons and pentagons. It is interesting to imagine, however, all of the possible polyhedra there are.

Many, many mathematicians (Euler, to name one of the more famous) have explored these ideas in much, much greater detail than this.   If your students are interested in doing so, simply search the World Wide Web for "Platonic Solids."

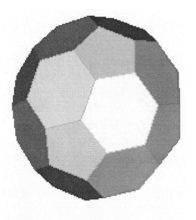

Problem #12
Hurricane Andrew and How Big is a Billion?

Hurricane Andrew caused $26 billion in damage, making it the most costly natural disaster in American history. How long would it take you to deal that much money in one-dollar bills? How tall would a stack of 26 billion one-dollar bills be?

Skills used:

Comprehending large numbers
interpreting data
converting units of time and distance
place value
exponents
scientific notation

This problem came from the National Council of Teachers of Mathematics' World's Largest Math Event 5. Originally, the figure was $20 billion. Some sources estimate the damage as high as $30 billion. I chose $26 million because the most extensive reports I read showed $25 billion in damages in Florida and another $1 billion in Louisiana.

This problem is a wonderful way to illustrate the enormity of large numbers like a million and a billion. We throw these terms around casually:

"There must have been a million people there."
"If I had a million dollars, I'd buy that."
"Things like that are one in a million."

Kids hear these numbers all the time. News reporters describe defense spending, national deficits, professional athletes' salaries, and music stars' record sales daily. Really, our brains can only visualize numbers that are much smaller. Think about it: Can you look at a group of people and accurately estimate how many people there are? Maybe when there are a dozen or so, but how about a cafeteria full? How about a stadium full?

I always begin this unit with the question, "What was the most expensive natural disaster in American history?" Students shout out all kinds of answers, including the attacks on New York City and the Pentagon in 2001. They call out earthquakes and wildfires. In particular, because I teach in Louisiana, they name several major hurricanes: Audrey, Hugo, Camille. Usually, someone names Andrew. I have a presentation on my computer with some pictures of the damage caused by Andrew that I show. Once we've determined that Andrew is the culprit, I pose the first question.

It's fun to let the kids guess at the answer first. I almost never get a guess anywhere near the answer.

You can let kids brainstorm about how to begin the problem, or you can tell them that the first thing to do is find out how fast money can be dealt. Depending on how you want to pace the lesson, you can allow them to determine this on their own, or you can do what I do and provide a deck of playing cards and have one student deal a number of cards in front of the class while we time it with a stopwatch. The benefit of this is that all students will be working with the same data, instead of individual times.

I usually allow the class some freedom by letting them decide how many cards we'll deal. Some want the whole deck, some say 10 cards are enough, and once in a while, someone with some vision wants 26 cards. If you use a number other than 26, it will be more difficult, but that's not necessarily a bad thing.

In my class, it took Tiffany 11 seconds to deal 26 cards. As a class, we came up with the notion that 26 cards in 11 seconds means 26 billion cards in 11 billion seconds. That's really the answer – 11,000,000,000 seconds, but I insist on a "useful" answer. I mean, I don't know how long that is. I know it's longer than a couple of minutes. I'll usually turn the students loose to work on their own or in small groups at this point. I definitely distribute calculators, preferably graphing calculators or other calculators that display several calculations at once.

To a grown-up, the obvious solution is to divide 11,000,000,000 by 60 because there are 60 seconds in a minute. To middle schoolers, this doesn't jump out quite so quickly sometimes. If it does, great. If not, you may have to ask, "How many minutes is that?" This comes out to about 183,333,333 minutes. Whether the students are allowed to round this off to 183 million is up to you. I usually encourage rounding because you're dealing with a fictional situation anyway. I mean, no one deals 26 billion dollars out, so precision here is kind of moot. If Tiffany could deal 2 more cards per second, the final answer would be extremely different. In fact, you may get big differences from one class to the next. The kids will get hung up on getting an exact answer; they don't even like dividing by 365 because of leap years! This is a good chance to illustrate the use of estimation: In addition to making some calculations easier, estimation sometimes is just smart because you really don't know what the real numbers are. Why work hard to calculate with difficult numbers when they aren't the right numbers anyway?

183,333,333 minutes divided by 60 (because there are 60 minutes in an hour) yields about 3,055,555 or about 3,000,000 hours. Three million hours!

3 million hours divided by 24 (hours in a day) gives you about 127,000 days. That's still incomprehensible, but if you think of 1,000 days as almost three years, you can begin to visualize the magnitude of the answer.

127,000 days divided by 365 (days in a year) equals around 347 years! Wow! That's incredible! 347 years ago, there wasn't even a United States of America! 347 years from now, there may not be a United States of America.

I find that students often don't want to divide by 365 in this last step. They want to find weeks or months because they fail to see that 127,000 days is going to be so big. This is a result (I think) of over-reliance on calculators. The kids see a big number on the calculator but don't really stop to look at it. Let them calculate weeks and months; there's no better way to learn than experience.

One of my 7th graders, Zach, had a different way of looking at the problem. Zach's number sense was very strong at basic (addition and subtraction) levels, but he had missed out on some major developmental opportunities in the upper elementary grades. Zach knew that there were 60 seconds in a minute, so he punched in 60 on his calculator. He then added 60 to get 120, or the number of seconds in two minutes. He proceeded to continue to add 60 over and over again, but kept losing track of his count. I showed him how to use the enter key on his calculator to add repeatedly. I decided not to share the big secret of multiplication with him just yet. Once he had hit the enter key 60 times, he knew that there were 3600 seconds in an hour. He then added 3600 repeatedly, counting keystrokes until he reached 24. He then knew there were 86,400 seconds in a day. I then showed him that 3600 times 24 was 86,400. He still wanted to count keystrokes, though, so 365 strokes later, he arrived at 31,536,000 seconds in a year. He wasn't quite sure what to do with this huge number, so we talked for a minute. He decided to add this number repeatedly until he reached 11 billion, and then he'd know how many years it took.

Sure enough, Zach pressed that enter key 350 times. He kept getting help reading what number his calculator had reached. Once it got into the billions, the calculator went into scientific notation, with the first two digits reading 1.0. He figured out that once he got to 1.1, he'd be there!

Once the students begin to appreciate the enormity of $26,000,000,000, it's time for question number two: How tall would a stack of $26,000,000 in one-dollar bills be? Again, the guesses are far short. Some students demonstrate a stack of money as tall as their heads. Some will compare the stack to a tall building, like the World Trade Center towers, especially with the events of September 2001 so recent.

Firstly, we need to determine how tall a smaller stack of paper is. You can measure a ream of paper, some pages out of a textbook, or some real money. Failing any of that, the U.S. Department of the Treasury measures a stack of 50 bills at 0.215 inches, or 0.55 centimeters. Although the Treasury's measurement will obviously be more accurate, it will be less meaningful than a measurement that students have made.

Students with some foresight will want to measure 26 or 260 pieces of paper so the math will be easy. If they have this much foresight, they have obviously done enough difficult math in their lives to see the need for this shortcut. Don't make them do a difficult calculation.

Again, the final answer needs to be "useful." For this example, we'll use the Treasury's measurement. 26,000,000,000 divided by 50 equals 520,000,000. So there are 520 million stacks of fifty, each stack being 0.215 inches tall. 0.215 times 520 million is 111,800,000 inches tall for the stack. To turn this into a useful number, we divide by 12 for feet. This yields 9,316,666 feet.

With a little vision, students will see that this number is many miles, since a mile is only 5280 feet. So we divide 9,316,666 by 5280 to get 1764 miles.

1764 miles! Are you kidding? Wait a minute, that's pretty high, but still incomprehensible. Is that taller than the World Trade Center towers were? Is that as far as the moon? Can airplanes go that high?

Well, the World Trade Center towers were just a little over ¼ of a mile high. So is the Sears Tower in Chicago (1450 ft.) and so are the Petronas Towers in Kuala Lumpur, Malaysia (1483 ft.). Most airliners fly at around 30,000 feet and the SR-71 Blackbird flew in excess of 85,000 feet, which is about 16 miles. The moon is 240,000 miles away, so our stack is way taller than the tallest building, much higher than an airplane could fly, but nowhere near the distance of the moon.

Let's imagine that we took that stack of money and laid it on its side. It's 1764 miles long! Using any map of America, we can see that is about halfway across the contiguous states. Use your town as a starting point and map it out. Maybe one of your students has driven that distance. It's so far that most people stop and spend the night in a hotel once or twice when driving it! In my classroom, we imagine the drive from South Louisiana to California or to Maine.

It's fun to verbalize to kids: "Imagine that when you wake up in the morning, there are one-dollar bills from your room to the kitchen. Not lined up end to end, but stacked on their sides. The money continues outside and to the street, and then all the way to school. If you stopped to pick it all up, you'd fill up your house and need more room. The money continues down the street and onto the highway and all the way to the next town, an hour away. If you kept on driving, with this money stacked on the side of the road where you could look out of your window at it the whole way, you'd have to stop at a hotel for sleep a couple of times before you saw the end of it."

So there it is. There are a lot of extensions and side conversations you could implement. For example, the September 11, 2001 disaster in New York was probably more costly than Hurricane Andrew. Some sources quote the insurance loss at about $19 billion, but the overall loss at over $90 billion. Estimates place the technological infrastructure of Wall Street alone at a $3.2 billion dollar rebuild.

Sometimes, especially with younger children, it is a good idea to start smaller, with only one million. If you have the technology, you can program an old computer or a graphing calculator to count to a million and have kids predict when it will get there. If you use an old computer that uses the BASIC programming language, here's the program:

```
10 LET A = 1
20 PRINT A
30 LET A = A + 1
40 GOTO 20
```

The above program is simple and will count past a million. It will count indefinitely. If you want it to stop at a million, the program should look like this:

```
10 LET A = 1
20 PRINT A
30 LET A = A + 1
40 IF A = 1000001 THEN GOTO 60
50 GOTO 20
60 END
```

If you use the Texas Instruments series of graphing calculator, the program looks like this:

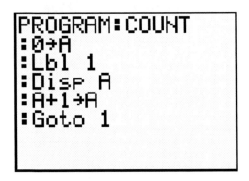

```
PROGRAM:COUNT
:0→A
:Lbl 1
:Disp A
:A+1→A
:Goto 1
```

Kids really enjoy record-setters, like tallest buildings, richest people, fastest jet planes, etc. Knowing this, I can't resist sharing with them some really huge numbers. (The caret, or $^\wedge$, represents an exponent.)

1,000,000 = 10$^\wedge$6 = 1 million
1,000,000,000 = 10$^\wedge$9 = 1 billion
1,000,000,000,000 = 10$^\wedge$12 = 1 trillion
1,000,000,000,000,000 = 10$^\wedge$15 = 1 quadrillion
1,000,000,000,000,000,000 = 10$^\wedge$18 = 1 quintillion
1,000,000,000,000,000,000,000 = 10$^\wedge$21 = 1 sextillion
10$^\wedge$24 = 1 septillion
10$^\wedge$27 = 1 octillion
10$^\wedge$30 = 1 nonillion
10$^\wedge$33 = 1 decillion

10^36 = 1 undecillion
10^39 = 1 duodecillion
10^42 = 1 tredecillion
10^45 = 1 quattuordecillion
10^48 = 1 quindecillion
10^51 = 1 sexdecillion
10^54 = 1 septendecillion
10^57 = 1 octodecillion
10^60 = 1 novemdecillion
10^63 = 1 vigintillion
10^66 = 1 unvigintillion
10^69 = 1 dovigintillion
10^72 = 1 trevigintillion
10^75 = 1 quattuorvigintillion
10^78 = 1 quinvigintillion
10^81 = 1 sexvigintillion
10^84 = 1 septenvigintillion
10^87 = 1 octovigintillion
10^90 = 1 novemvigintillion
10^93 = 1 trigintillion
10^96 = 1 untrigintillion
10^99 = 1 duotrigintillion

Some scientists estimate 10^80 to be the number of subatomic particles in the known universe. That's electrons, protons, and all that stuff!

The numbers can be named in a like manner forever. This is only the American way of naming numbers. If your students are interested, they can research how other countries name these numbers. Here are some more large ones:

10^100 = 1 googol = a 1 with 100 zeroes
10^303 = 1 centillion = a 1 with 303 zeroes or 3.03 googol
10^googol = 1 googolplex = a 1 with a googol zeroes

A googolplex is far larger than any of the numbers listed here and spurs one to think about infinity and what infinity means. One source says that a googolplex, printed in 12-point font, would stretch from here to Pluto and back six times. Another illustration of hugeness: The largest prime number known to date is expressed as 2^13,466,917-1, contains 4,053,946 digits and would take the best part of three weeks to write out longhand. It would stretch about 4 miles when written out in small print and well over 100 miles if written in large print on a chalk board or dry-erase board.

Problem #13
Lotsa Cubes

Investigate what happens when different-sized cubes are constructed from unit cubes, the surface area is painted and the large cube is then disassembled into its original unit cubes. How many of the 1x1x1 cubes are painted on three faces, two faces, one face, and no faces? Develop a rule for finding these numbers on any size cube.

Skills Used:

Area
Volume
Perimeter
Surface Area
Finding patterns
identifying algebraic relationships
graphing equations

Before the students have learned what surface area is, but after they have learned area, I have them construct a 2x2x2 cube out of small wooden cubes. I ask, "If I spray painted your cube, including the bottom, how many square units of paint would I use?" Although most students look at this problem as 4x6, with 4 square units on each face of the cube, some may look at it as 8x3, or 8 cubes, each with 3 faces painted.

Some kids will need to build a model of the first few stages of this problem. Some will want to draw a model. I find that many middle schoolers are amazed at my ability to draw a cube, so I use this opportunity to show them how.

First, draw a square:

Next, draw three parallel segments leaving the top two corners and the bottom right one:

Now connect the ends of those segments:
It doesn't even have to be a good looking cube, as long as you can use your model.

Dimensions	#of 1x1x1 cubes needed	# of unit cubes with paint on			
		3 faces	2 faces	1 face	0 faces
2x2x2	8	8	0	0	0
3x3x3	27	8	12	6	1
4x4x4	64	8	24	24	8
5x5x5	125	8	36	54	27
.	.	.	.	.	.
.	.	.	.	.	.
.	.	.	.	.	.
nxnxn	n^3	8	$12(n-2)$	$6(n-2)^2$	$(n-2)^3$

Students can usually see pretty quickly that the corner pieces, which have three faces painted, will always equal 8. They can also determine that the number of pieces with two faces painted goes up by 12 every time, but have trouble finding where the 12 is in the model. The 12 represents the number of edges. Each of the 12 edges has a group of small cubes that have 2 faces painted. The size of that group depends on the size of the cube. Whatever the side length of the cube is, the group of two-faced cubes is two less because of the two corner pieces with three faces painted.

The cubes with only one face painted is a little trickier. A student might realize that the pattern is 6,24,54, ... which is 6x1, 6x4, 6x9,...

I had a student realize this part of the problem by sketching only the front of each large cube and shading the pieces with only one face painted. She knew that the result would have to be multiplied by 6 because of the 6 faces of the cube. By drawing this out, she could see that each square face of the cube had a smaller square shaded on it and was able to piece together the rule.

Students can often (but not always) figure out that the number of unpainted cubes (in the middle of the large cube) is a cubic number, but can't get the rule for it. The rule is very similar to the rules for the other small cubes.

Problem #14
Planting Trees

How can you plant 10 trees in five rows with four trees in each row?

This is one of those problems that really builds thinkers, but has little that is measurable, so be warned: if your lesson plan must show what standards and benchmarks you are teaching, you may want to avoid this problem. If, on the other hand, you're looking for a good brain-builder that almost all students can solve, this is it!

This problem would be a good one to begin your school year with, introducing the students to your procedures for group work. It would also be a good activity on those days when you know class is not going to go the way it should: half the class is going to leave in the middle because of a field trip or it is the day before Christmas holidays or your school is having a program. There aren't really any major concepts that your students need to be taught; anyone with a little persistence has the potential to solve this one.

Of course, students think this is either a trick question or that it is impossible. If they don't, they probably aren't paying close enough attention. Make sure the students realize that there are three qualifiers that have to all happen to make a solution correct: 1) There must be 10 trees, 2) they must be in 5 rows, and 3) there must be 4 trees in each row. If any of these is not true, the solution is not correct. My students begin each year with a strong need for affirmation. All I really want to do on this problem is offer a little boost if a student is stumped, and monitor group discussions, but I am often asked, "Is this the answer?" My usual reply is "I don't know. Is it?" However, on problems like this, where the answer is not easy to find, but very easy to verify, I begin the activity with the rule that no one can ask me if their answer is correct.

One of the mental roadblocks to the problem is that students don't realize that one tree can be in two different rows. Here is a diagram of seven trees in two rows of four:

o o o

o

o

o

This is a concept that you can bring out if you stop the groups after a few minutes and allow them to share their

thinking up until this point. Why should you say it if you can allow a student the chance to verbalize his or her thinking?

Once they realize that a tree can be on more than one row, students start constructing all sorts of arrangements, either by drawing or by using a model like poker chips.

The answer is that the ten trees lie on the vertices of two similar regular pentagons, with the smaller one inverted inside the larger. This is quite a mouthful, and it is probably more obvious that the trees lie on the line segments that form a star:

Here are some extensions of this problem:

Write your own problem for others to solve using the vertices of another type of polygon.

What shapes are formed when you connect vertices of different polygons?

This design has each tree as part of two rows. What design can you make with each tree as part of three rows?

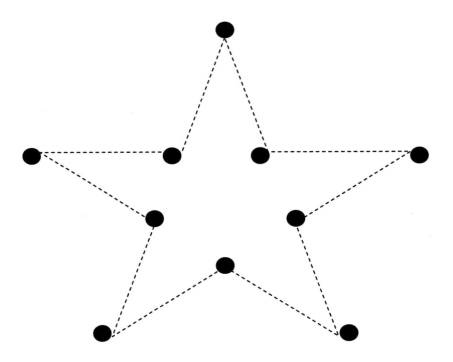

Problem #15
The Hollow Cube

A hollow cube has a volume of .027 cubic meters. If it is opened and laid flat as in the picture, what is the area of the resulting figure? What is its perimeter?

Here it is! Perimeter, area, and volume all in one problem! Other skills students can use in just this problem: Adding, multiplying and dividing decimals, finding cube roots, and understanding exponents.

Is it too hard for your 5th or 6th graders? Just change the volume to an easier number, like 8 cubic meters or even 1 cubic meter. Too easy for your 8th or 9th graders? Change the volume to a harder cube, like 1331 cubic meters or to a non-cube, like 750 cubic meters. Or require the answer in another unit of measurement, like inches or kilometers.

The solution is that you take the cube root of the volume (in this case it's .3) and that is the side length. Multiply the side length by 14 for the perimeter, which is 4.2 m. Square the side length (multiply it by itself) to get .09 and multiply that by 6 to get the area, .54 square meters.

The question to ask if you're not teaching cube roots is, "What number times itself three times is .027?"

This problem is a great refresher for students who have already learned about area, perimeter, and volume. It is a great introduction to cube roots for older students.

If you're one of those unusual teachers, give this problem to students before they know what area, perimeter, and volume are and let them figure it out using the glossary and the explanations in the textbook. This is fun in a gifted class.

I find that students often can't remember which is area and which is perimeter, and which is volume. They have been taught the formulas for each, but because the formulas are just abstract bits of data crammed into their memories, they can't recall them effectively.

I am reminded of a story I heard at NCTM's annual meeting in 2002. The speaker received a phone call from a woman who hadn't seen him since high school. The woman had been a competent student in high school mathematics, always doing just enough for a good grade, but never really attempting any deep understanding. After the introduction, she began the conversation with:

> *Caller: You were always good at math, right?*
> *Speaker: Yes.*
> *Caller: Well, I'm trying to hang wallpaper.*
> *Speaker: OK.*
> *Caller: It says on the package to find the area and divide by 25 and that's how many rolls to buy, but I don't think I have enough rolls. I multiplied length times width to get the area.*
> *Speaker: Well, you have enough wallpaper to cover either the ceiling or the floor.*
> *Caller: Huh?*
> *Speaker: To get the area of the wall, you have to multiply the length of the wall by its height.*
> *Caller: Height? That's in the volume formula!*

She was such a good student that ten years later, she still had the formulas memorized, but she had no idea what they really meant. Our students are the same way, but we can catch them now, instead of ten years after high school.

One trick I have seen many times and used myself is to get students to remember that the word perimeter has the word RIM in it. Many teachers have their students write the word perimeter with the word RIM capitalized, like this: peRIMeter. This works for some students.

Another memory aid I use is to tell a good story about my time in the Army when we had to form a perimeter around something or when we had to conduct an area reconnaissance to search an entire area for enemy activity.

You can talk about how shampoo gives your hair volume, which is three-dimensional space, or how an area rug covers a two-dimensional area.

Learners who like to be organized will appreciate a chart showing that perimeter is measured in linear units, area is measured in square units, and volume is measured in cubic units. I like to take some rulers (they are usually inexpensive) and tape one ruler to the wall with a sign that says "one linear foot." Then I tape 4 rulers in a square shape to the wall with a sign that says "one square foot." Then I hang from the ceiling 12 rulers taped together as the edges of a cube with a sign that says "one cubic foot."

A fun activity to do to help students remember is to have them measure their own linear, square, and cubic measurements.

First, trace each student on a large piece of paper. They always love this! Have them measure and record their height. This is a linear measurement. It is one-dimensional. Now have them measure their perimeter. They'll probably need a piece of string that they can bend to follow their outline. This measurement will be much longer than their height, but it's still linear and one-dimensional. The string (or the pencil outline) has no real width – just length. (Of course, it really has width, but when we speak of a line mathematically, it doesn't.)

Then, have the students find the area of their outline. They can do this by using graph paper squares or 1-inch tiles or whatever you can think of, but they'll have to estimate the partial squares on the curved parts of their outline.

Then, have students find their volume. This is tricky and will require some advance preparation. Get a large box (like a refrigerator or washing machine might come in) and almost fill it with Styrofoam peanuts. Measure the volume of the peanuts by measuring the length, height, and width of the peanut-filled portion of the box and multiplying them. Immerse a student in the peanuts and measure the new, greater volume. Subtract the two and you've got the volume of the student!

You still want more? Get with the science teacher and teach density and have kids use their volume and weight to find their density. What is water's density? Would you float on water?

Hang the outlines and data in the hall, share it on math night, print digital pictures of kids' faces in the computer lab and paste them on the outlines, or whatever, but make the activity memorable enough and the kids won't forget these valuable definitions that so often end up gathering dust in the recesses of the brain.

Reproducible Worksheets

The following pages are provided for easy reproduction. Since this book is 8.5 inches by 5.5 inches, you may turn it sideways on a copier to reproduce these pages, leaving lots of blank space where students can write.

Name _____   Date _____

Hose A can fill the bucket in 45 minutes. Hose B can do the same in 30 minutes. How long will it take both hoses together to fill the bucket?

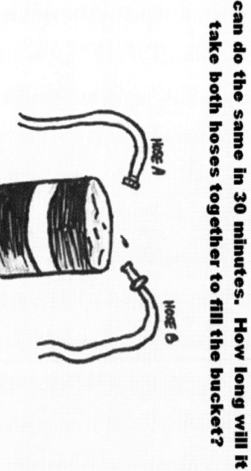

Explain your thinking below:

In the diagram below, how many "C" balls does it take to balance one "A" ball?

Explain your thinking below:

Name _____   Date _____

If you take a lot of small cubes, put them together to form a large cube, paint the large cube, and disassemble the cube into the smaller cubes again, how many of the small cubes will have paint on three faces? Two faces? One face? No faces? Complete the table below.

Dimensions	# of 1x1x1 cubes needed	# of unit cubes with paint on			
		3 faces	2 faces	1 face	0 faces
2x2x2	8	8	0	0	0
3x3x3	27	8	12	6	1
4x4x4	64	8	24	24	8
5x5x5	125	8	36	54	27
10x10x10					
20x20x20					
75x75x75					
nxnxn					

Name _____   Date _____

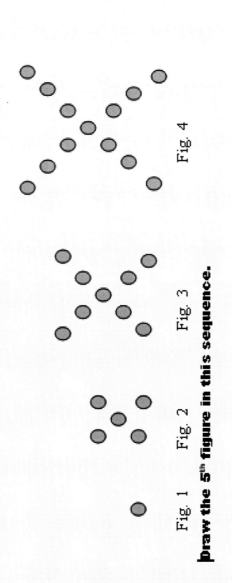

Fig. 1   Fig. 2   Fig. 3   Fig. 4

Draw the 5th figure in this sequence.

How many dots are in the 23rd figure? _____

How many dots are in the 98th figure? _____

How many dots are in the nth figure? _____

Explain your reasoning.

About the Author

Andrew Field has taught middle school mathematics since 1996. He holds a Bachelor of Arts degree in elementary education from Northwestern State University in Natchitoches, Louisiana. A member of the National Council of Teachers of Mathematics, he was one of six national recipients of the Mathematics Education Trust's Future Leaders Award in 2002.

He is married to the former Kate Herrington and they live in Natchitoches, Louisiana with their three daughters, Evelyn, Corinne, and Lydia.

The author at an undisclosed location with one million dollars in $100 bills during Operation Iraqi Freedom (See Hurricane Andrew and How Big is a Billion?).

ISBN 141201509-X

350050